MANAGING BY ACCOUNTABILITY

MANAGING BY ACCOUNTABILITY

What Every Leader Needs to Know about

Responsibility, Integrity—and Results

M. David Dealy
with Andrew R. Thomas

Westport, Connecticut
London

Library of Congress Cataloging-in-Publication Data

Dealy, M. David.
    Managing by accountability : what every leader needs to know about
    responsibility, integrity–and results / M. David Dealy with Andrew R. Thomas.
       p.   cm.
    Includes bibliographical references and index.
    ISBN 0–275–99332–9 (alk. paper)
    1. Management.   2. Responsibility.   3. Business ethics.   4. Leadership.
I. Thomas, Andrew R.   II. Title.
    HD31.D377   2007
    658.4′092–dc22   2006028566

British Library Cataloguing in Publication Data is available.

Library of Congress Catalog Card Number: 2006028566
ISBN: 0–275–99332–9

First published in 2007

Praeger Publishers, 88 Post Road West, Westport, CT 06881
An imprint of Greenwood Publishing Group, Inc.
www.praeger.com

Printed in the United States of America

The paper used in this book complies with the
Permanent Paper Standard issued by the National
Information Standards Organization (Z39.48–1984).

10 9 8 7 6 5 4 3 2 1

To Rob Krebs,
Thanks for teaching me about accountability . . . from
all sides.

Contents

Chapter 1

The Mandate of Accountability

Watch your thoughts; they become words. Watch your words; they become actions. Watch your actions; they become habits. Watch your habits; they become character. Watch your character; it becomes your destiny.

Frank Outlaw

ONE OF MY FIRST JOBS in the railroad industry was as superintendent of a terminal in the western United States. I was viewed by my superiors as an up-and-comer and given a responsibility that was normally held for people who had been in the business for at least fifteen years. I was told by my boss that the situation where I was going would be rough and chaotic. When I first assumed my duties, I was shocked to find things were much worse. The inventory was strewn everywhere. Any administrative activity was a hindrance, not a help. Morale among the team was low. In short, things were in real, real bad shape.

After a few weeks of trying my best, I believed progress was being made, although slowly. Then one day, unannounced, I got a call from my boss that said the "Big Boss" was coming in the next day for a visit. Scared and excited, I made every effort to put on a good show for the visiting VIP.

From the moment he arrived, it was clear to the Big Boss that things were on the verge of spinning out of control. Every item he asked to see was even less impressive than the previous one. After exasperatingly observing more and more disorder, the Big Boss finally turned to me and said, "Dave, tell me what I've witnessed here is just the product of a bad day. Assure me that yesterday things were better. And, that if I were to come back tomorrow, I would see an improved operation."

"No," I said. "It is clear things here are not running very well. Yesterday was a bit worse than today and I can only hope tomorrow will be better."

I continued, "I realize it is my responsibility to run this operation and that the buck stops with me. I can only promise you that I will do my best to improve things."

His silent response was most disconcerting, as I was now firmly convinced that my future with this company was ruined.

After the traditional dinner that night and a brief meeting the following morning, it was time for the Big Boss to depart. At the send-off, he pulled me aside and put his arm around me. He told me he was extremely happy with what he saw during his visit. The Big Boss then said something that has stuck with me the rest of my life:

> Dave, I can train almost anybody to run a railway yard. Inventory management and administration are processes that are important, but they can be taught and learned. However, I cannot teach anyone how to hold themselves accountable.

At its core, accountability is really the responsibility to act. And, based on my nearly thirty years in industry, accountability is something that must first come from within. Dishearteningly, however, this is many times the opposite of what is happening today in corporate America.

Now don't get me wrong. I understand that accountability is certainly in vogue today. Everywhere we find people screaming for it. Everyday more and more companies are signing up to the challenge of improving and communicating with their stakeholders, yet the same questions seemingly keep coming back again and again:

- Why do we have to go through all this change?

- When is someone going to train me?

- Who dropped the ball?

- Why can't they communicate better?

- When is that department going to do its job right?

- Who's going to solve the problem?

- When am I going to find good people?

- Why don't they share the vision?

- Who's going to clarify my job?

Dishearteningly, when we do get accountability, it usually is a watered-down version of what is really needed. Moreover, those entrusted with responsibilities often wait for some third party or outside mechanism to do something before accountability is unleashed. In some cases it may be Congress, the media, the legal department, Wall Street, or some other entity that forces accountability.

This is not to say that formal accountability programs are wasteful or have no place within society. They play an important role. And we'll talk about some in the later pages of this book.

Nevertheless, it is ultimately the individual who holds themselves to the highest standard first—without waiting to be told, pushed, or prodded to accountability—that leads the best.

James McNerney, the former Chairman and CEO, 3M Co., and now CEO of Boeing Corporation, is undoubtedly one of the stars in the business world. His ability to lead an organization on the principles of personal integrity, accountability, responsibility, and results are legendary. Here are some of McNerney's words of wisdom as they relate to what managers must do when it comes to holding themselves to the highest of standards:

> The fact is, demands on business leaders have increased exponentially. Leadership development is the single most important element to sustained success. We believe that good leaders start with the premise that very often the most relevant knowledge exists either at the bottom or outside their organizations. And the leader's task is to encourage people to bring that knowledge forward, learn from it and act on it.[1]

Those who successfully manage by accountability viscerally know that external rules cannot substitute for character. That holding oneself accountable is an acquirement—like music, like a foreign language, like poker. Nobody is born with it. Managing by accountability evolves over time within us. Accountability offers something better than success. It provides a measure of whether you are doing the best you can in the circumstances at hand.

So Where Did This All Start?

The word *accountability* in English comes from the fourteenth-century word *accounts*, meaning a record of money received and paid. King James II of England was the first to publicly use the term *accountability*. In 1688, he said to his people, "I am accountable for all things that I openly and voluntarily do or say." In short, the word means being answerable for your actions. It does not necessarily mean you will succeed. James lost his throne within a year of making his pledge.

It is because of human nature that we have such a thing as accountability. People are not so committed to a cause that they all just naturally do what they should. Organizations would always be needed (even in a utopian society) in order to work out group consensus on things. But they are needed for more than that. Because of human nature, you cannot count on each member leaving a meeting and all carrying out their responsibilities faithfully. People forget. They get sidetracked. They lose interest, slack off, and just plain shirk their responsibilities. So that is where accountability comes in.

But Here's a Problem . . .

How rarely do you hear someone in any arena of society voluntarily step forward early in any form of catastrophe and say, "X was my fault! That was my responsibility! I am accountable for this failure! I am to blame! And this is how I am going to fix it!" Such happens so rarely that our society is quite skeptical if such acknowledgments occur.

In our society, it is many times considered foolish to acknowledge responsibility and accountability. To do so is to open one's self to law suits and perhaps criminal charges! Certainly, there are many relevant factors in any disaster. Consider how we frequently approach catastrophic happenings. "Who will 'take the fall' for this?" "Who will we make the 'scapegoat'?" "Where will we place the blame—on a person or a circumstance?" "How will we manage damage control?"

This is also quite evident in the most personal of matters. For example, when a marriage fails, frequently she says, "It is his fault! If he would change Y, we would have no serious problems. Our marriage has failed because he refuses to accept his responsibility!" He frequently says, "It is her fault! If she would change Z, we would have no serious problems. Our marriage has failed because she refuses to accept her responsibility!" In matters of personal relationships, we are quite adept at giving 100 percent blame to someone else.

Thus, rather than admitting "my" part in the matter, we learn to evade any sense of blame. We see this in our children from a very early age. They blame the dog for eating their homework, somebody sleeping in the house for why they couldn't clean their room for fear of waking them up, or the "magic man" who empties the orange juice carton and puts it back in the refrigerator instead of throwing it away.

Clearly, every situation is unique and should be approached as such—few things "are true of everyone" in a given situation. Yet, when a person dies from cancer caused by smoking, are tobacco companies 100 percent responsible? Was individual choice in no way responsible? Was the person powerless to make a choice? Who is accountable?

If drinking destroys my liver, can 100 percent of the blame be put on the brewery? What role did individual choice play in producing a horrific consequence? Do individual "rights" mean it is the responsibility of a government agency to protect me from every situation in life? Who is accountable?

Certainly, these are complex questions. Never is justice done in any situation by oversimplifying the matter. For sure, no one or no group has "a license" to ignore human well-being by producing a dangerous product designed to exploit human addiction. No one or no group has the right to reduce a woman to a "thing to be used" and violently disregard her person. Surely, each person should be respected as an individual. The objective of these questions is not to suggest otherwise.

The matter to consider is this: choices and our decisions produce consequences. When bad consequences result from a choice made, we are not served well by seeking to absolve ourselves or others through trying to place 100 percent of the blame on other people or the circumstances. If that is the course we choose to take, then (1) we learn little or nothing from experiencing the consequence and become likely to make the same mistake again, (2) those around us learn little or nothing positive from the experience except that we are not to be completely trusted, (3) our ability to lead is seriously weakened, and (4) bad things are bound to happen.

In 1995, the oldest bank in England that preached integrity and accountability as its mantra for decades, announced it was seeking bankruptcy. It lost nearly $1 billion in a stock gamble. At the time it went under, it held over $100 million in assets for Queen Elizabeth. A year earlier, the chief trader at their Singapore office started betting some very big money on Japan's stock market. He made a lot of money for the company, but then an earthquake hit Kobe, Japan, and in January 1995, the stock market took a severe nosedive.

Thinking it was a very temporary loss, the trader started doubling up on his gambling, hoping to make very large sums when the market rebounded. Instead of the bank cutting its losses, it just kept pouring money into the Singapore exchange and their employee would just use it to bet more on the market. They sent nearly $900 million to this man, and he, in turn, lost it all.

How could one twenty-eight-year-old employee in Singapore lose nearly a billion dollars and ruin the oldest and most influential bank in England? It all boiled down to a lack of supervision. Who was accountable?

A Culture of Accountability in a World of Teams

For employees to be accountable there must be an environment and a culture of accountability, and that comes from those above them. Nevertheless, the reality of business today is that many organizations tend to favor a horizontal management structure over a vertical one. To deal with the complexities of global pressures and real-time expectations, matrices and ad hoc structures are often intertwined. Folks from across the organizations become members of teams where roles and responsibilities are temporary and lines of traditional management structures are blurred.

Many organizations hope—somehow, some way—that in these kinds of situations, the best outcomes will be reached through mutual accountability. The result is usually a complete lack of accountability, with decisions being dominated by stronger personalities and conflict avoided.

Conflict is inevitable in an organization; knowledge workers with strong personalities and opinions are going to clash. A leader needs to be aware of this and understand how his or her organization is going to deal with it. Accountability is where it begins. Far too often, however, managers focus on trying to maintain a happy, family-based culture. They fail to realize that even functional and happy families disagree and argue.[2]

Reaching conclusions in a team through wide consultation is important, but eventually someone needs to own the process for each decision—experience has shown that to reach an optimal decision an individual needs to be held viciously accountable.

What This Book Is About

Despite the multitude of theory and opinion that an organization is a reflection of its people, ultimately an organization is a reflection of its leadership and their management methods. My earlier books on what constitutes a great boss and understanding how to take advantage of inevitable change each touched on the issue of accountability in a number of ways. In the following pages, I want to illustrate in greater detail how the role of personal accountability has shaped my career and that of many successful leaders whom I know. Also, I want to help guide you away from some of the most common mistakes that get made by those well-intentioned leaders who seek to manage by accountability.

Simply saying "I am accountable" and trying your best is not nearly enough. It is only the beginning. It is the beginning of a much larger process that will lead to greater effectiveness and results as a leader. Claiming accountability for something that has gone awry requires a personal commitment to see things through to a more positive outcome. This is not often easy, nor pleasant. Neither is being a leader.

In short, if we don't manage by accountability, we end up in the blame game and nothing good ever comes from that. On the other hand, if accountability is the benchmark and claimed when a situation requiring it arises, then there is good chance that improvements can be implemented and the problem ultimately solved. This requires action. And it can only begin when we truly understand the relationship between accountability and responsibility.

Chapter 2

The Relationship between Accountability and Responsibility—and Blame

Responsibility is to keep the ability to respond.
Robert Duncan

FEBRUARY 1, 1996, IS A DAY that will remain permanently seared into my mind, heart, and soul. I was in Springfield, Missouri, to perform a typical field operations audit. My pager went off just about the time I was walking into our office building. I called our operations center in the Chicago suburb of Schaumburg and spoke with Danny Reynolds, our General Superintendent. The conversation started out bad and got worse.

> Dave, I hate to be the one to have to tell you this, but one of our trains just made an emergency call from Cajon Pass. They said the train was out of control going down a steep grade and they were going to jump. That's all we know. We have alerted the police and ambulance teams and they are responding. All we can do now is wait.

This was unbelievable. How could this be happening? We had just had a runaway train accident at this same location a year earlier. One of our trains had lost its air brakes and had collided with a loaded coal train that was stopped ahead. The engineer and conductor had jumped seconds prior to impact at a speed we estimated was in excess of thirty-five miles per hour. The collision was horrific. The locomotives were engulfed in flames.

About fifteen minutes had passed since I had first spoken with Danny. I called him back on the hotline and I could sense a great degree of gravity in his voice. "We lost contact with the crew. We have received reports from the Sheriff that there was a large explosion with a big fireball. It looks like the entire train left the track and is in a pile. Our crew members are missing."

I quickly chartered a jet and flew the three hours to Ontario Airport in Southern California. When I finally arrived at the scene, I learned that the engineer had been rescued from the burning locomotive by nearby ranchers. The bodies of the other two crew members had been discovered near the wreckage. They were dead.

The entire site was closed to all but emergency response personnel. Just like the previous year, we had the interstate closed. The tracks run parallel to Interstate 15, which is the main route between Los Angeles and Las Vegas. Interstate 40 breaks off east of there at Barstow. This forms one of the major connections between the huge population mass of the Southwest and the Midwest. Our accident had it shut down. We were on national news and things were getting real tough. Moreover, I had seemingly all of the state and federal agencies—including the National Transportation Safety Board (NTSB), the Department of Transportation, and the California Public Utilities Commission—coming down on me trying to conclude what had happened.

Our engineer had been badly injured. We all wanted to talk to him, including the news media. To make matters worse, immediately after a closed-to-the-public NTSB briefing, a local politician, looking only to get his mug in front of the cameras, announced to the press that the engineer was at fault. His comments, although great fodder for the cameras, were disingenuous and simply not true.

The media feeding frenzy was insatiable. We had to move the engineer to three different hospitals and ended up checking him in at a fourth under a false name. We were able to speak to him long enough to understand that he was not at fault, but the fire with the media had already been lit. And, like the four locomotives and fifty-seven freight cars up on the mountain, it was blazing.

It is standard practice in major train wrecks not to comment on the cause. Many times it takes days to put the pieces together and by that time it is no longer news. We are used to saying that the cause is under investigation and letting the story die a natural death below the fold on page 10. However, this one was not going away. The interstate was closed for almost three days. Hundreds of thousands of commuters were inconvenienced. Days later, we were still front page and getting thirty seconds at the top of every hour on CNN.

The chief concern for me was our engineer. He was being blamed for an accident that killed two of his fellow employees, shut down a major highway artery for three days, and posed a serious contamination threat to one of America's largest metropolitan areas. Something needed to be done.

Despite the fact that standard procedure and jurisdictional protocol were against me, I believed that I had to act. I rented a ballroom at a nearby hotel and assembled all of our employees, their families, and the union leadership. I told this group that while the media had blamed our engineer, we had determined that he was not at fault. In fact, on the basis of what we knew at the time, we concluded that he had done everything he could have to stop the train. Just like the wreck that had occurred just over a year before, something had caused the train's brakes to fail on all but the cars nearest to the locomotives. This was most disconcerting, I explained, because in this case the train was equipped with a new piece of technology that should have allowed the brakes to be set from the rear of the train using a radio-controlled device. For some reason or reasons, unknown at that time, the new device was not functioning properly.

I stated repeatedly that our train crew was not responsible. We were not going to blame them. I related that our prayers were with the engineer and his family as well as the families of the two crewmen fatally injured in the accident.

In the immediate days and weeks following the accident, we attended funerals, picked up the wreckage, ran off the back-log of train traffic, cooperated with the NTSB and the various federal and state agencies, dealt with congressional investigations, and worked hard on developing a plan that would prevent this mistake from ever happening again.

On top of all that, the U.S. Department of Transportation (DOT) created its own committee to study what had happened and reduce the likelihood of something like this happening again. The committee consisted of myself, a representative from the United Transportation Union, and a DOT employee.

As time went by and we began to retrace the events one by one, it became clear that a set of management decisions years before had created the environment that ultimately led to this tragic series of events. In other words, the management of the railroad, of which I was a full-fledged member, was to a large extent responsible for what had happened.

My time came a couple of years after the accident when I was sent to Seattle to address 4,000 union members and tell them why it had happened. Already a bit nervous, needless to say, I walked into the hall and got even more concerned when I saw open microphones scattered among the audience. In my mind,

I was imagining an emotional union member using the mikes to stir up his brothers to the point where I might be vocally or physically shredded.

I walked up to the podium at the front of the room and waited what seemed like eternity for everyone to calm down. Then the room went completely silent. I cleared my throat and began to speak.

> In most railroad accidents, it is usually a broken signal, a poorly functioning wheel, or a track displacement that is the root cause. However, in the Cajon case, it wasn't any of these. It was in fact broken management. And, as the accident happened on my watch, I am accountable. It is now my responsibility to take action and fix the problems that led to the crash. I ask you for your help.

I paused and the silence was truly deafening. At the same time, a guy in the back of the room walked over to one of the microphones and began to speak.

He said, "In all the years I have worked for the railroad, this was the first time I have ever heard someone from management accept responsibility for a mistake."

He then asked the others in the room to join him in a round of applause, which spontaneously turned into a standing ovation.

It is critical to understand that, ultimately, people account, not intangible things like "corporations" and "governments." For every important responsibility, there is accountability. Accountability is the obligation to answer for the discharge of responsibilities that affect others in important ways. The answering is for intentions as well as results. Whenever someone has an important responsibility, they have an obligation to answer to stakeholders for their decisions.

The Three Options When Things Go Awry

In my nearly thirty-year career at almost all levels of the industry where I work, it seems that there are three possible ways events can unfold when something doesn't work out right:

Blame

This could be the result of the weather or something else completely outside of the control of those doing the job. Most of the time, however, blame gets directed to the wrong place: other people. It is what children do. And far too many adults as well. It is a waste of time. All it does is prolong the agony and exacerbate an already bad situation.

The federal, state, and local response to Hurricane Katrina is a great example of the blame game in action. Although everybody knew the storm was a potential Category 5 and it was headed to New Orleans—where it was widely known for decades that the levees around the city could only withstand a Category 3—leaders at every level failed to be prepared for such a scenario. I remember watching television—2 days after the storm thrashed the Gulf Coast while corpses were still floating in the streets—and hearing city, state, and federal leaders and their teams of handlers begin to set the stage for the blame game.

The city folks said the federal folks didn't do what they were supposed to. The federal leaders said the state leaders blocked every effort for their assistance. They said we couldn't have imagined the levees were going to break. (I really like it when someone blames the lack of imagination. That's a good one.) And it went on and on and on . . . ad nauseum.

So while the amount of human suffering was in many ways increasing across the disaster zone, those who had the authority, resources, and responsibility to do something positive to help alleviate the situation ended up spending an inordinate amount of time playing the blame game.

A few months later, I remember watching Super Bowl XL between the Seattle Seahawks and the Pittsburgh Steelers. Not a fan of either team, I, like tens of millions of others, tuned in to watch for the spectacle of it all—and the commercials. As the game unfolded, it was clear that Seattle was not doing very well in its execution. Moreover, there were also some questionable calls by the referees that seemingly went against them. However, after the game, Seattle coach Mike Holmgren and many of his players focused their comments squarely on the referees and blamed the officials for their loss by a score of 21–10.

It appeared to me as absurd as it was shameful. Certainly the officials made at least one indisputable mistake. Matt Hasselbeck's tackle of Ike Taylor was not an illegal below-the-knee block. This and other uncertain calls had Coach Holmgren and his players frenetic after the loss.

Interestingly, they were quick not to mention the fumble by the Seahawks receiver that was called an incomplete pass. Pittsburgh was the only other team that could have recovered from that fumble. And Seattle's folks didn't bother to detail the two field goals they missed, how they botched the end-of-the-half time management, and their three holding penalties. Nor did they discuss their poor play calling. Was that the officials' fault as well? Losers make alibis and play the blame game.

This was in stark contrast to what I remember Greg Norman doing after his monumental collapse at the 1996 Masters Golf Tournament. Six strokes ahead at the start of the final day, Norman had what almost everyone believed was an insurmountable lead. It was going to be a great day for the world's number one ranked player as he marched to his first major championship. . . .

After eleven holes, the insurmountable had been wiped out and then the whole golfing world watched Norman as he self-destructed by going into the water for double bogey fives on both the twelfth and sixteenth holes. Nick Faldo held his nerve and ended up winning by an incredible five strokes. It was the biggest last-day turnaround in the sixty-year history of the tournament.

Norman carded a sad 78 and was just barely able to hang on to second place by a stroke. It was the eighth time Norman had finished as a runner-up in golf's four major championships. Golf fans will also recall how Norman lost some other major championships that looked like were going his way. He was the one in the lead when Larry Mize dramatically chipped in at the 1987 Masters, and Bob Tway holed his bunker shot to take the 1986 PGA title.

At the press conference after the tournament, I remember watching the world's number one player not mince words about his display and avoid the blame game.

"I played like s***," were his first words.

"It was all my mistakes. I didn't do the right things and Nick played great. I got a good old arse-whipping."

"Of course, I am disappointed. I put all the blame on myself. I am a winner, but I just didn't win today."

Accountability

To me, accountability is best encapsulated as follows:

"It happened on my watch, so therefore I am accountable."

If, like Greg Norman and unlike the Seattle Seahawks, we choose to avoid the blame game, the path to accountability becomes open to us. This is often where the "tipping point" lies when something is not quite right. Do we stay in the gutter and accomplish nothing or do we try to make a bad situation better?

Accountability is the realization and recognition that I am accountable for the results and outcomes. If accountability becomes my response to a particular situation, then there exists the possibility to right the ship and effectively solve the problem or problems that caused the situation. If the blame game, finger pointing, and name calling take over, the situation will further degenerate into a battle for self-survival. I will accomplish nothing and further reduce my effectiveness as a leader.

But as I said in the last chapter, stating accountability simply for the sake of avoiding the blame game is itself destructive. Real leaders who manage by accountability also know that there is a responsibility to do something to make things better and achieve results. And that is the other direction to head when things get off track.

Responsibility

After assuming accountability ("It happened on my watch"), the leader is now front and center in solving the problem and making sure it doesn't happen again. This means action!

From where I sit, a lot of the people who are in positions of authority are afraid to make decisions. They don't want to screw up, be embarrassed, or displease their boss. So they do little or nothing. And you know who sees that clearer than anybody else, the people who work for them!

I've seen a lot of lousy managers over my career who offend, unfairly criticize, or alienate their subordinates. Yet, it never ceases to amaze how when even someone like this makes a decision—whether the decision is a good one, a marginal one, or a determination of even terrible impact—the respect level for that same manager often goes way up. For merely possessing the attribute and ability to make a decision, the esteem of that leader rises in the eyes of those around them, despite their other baggage.

It's what we do that counts. Not what we don't do. Taking action and making decisions are an open window into what we are about as people and as leaders. Making decisions defines our value and benchmarks our credibility. Claiming the mantra of accountability means the responsibility to act. And act well. Failing to do so makes the leader a paper tiger and a hypocrite. The kind of leader people snicker at under their breath during a meeting and laugh about after it's over.

In order to be an effective, results-oriented leader, accountability and responsibility must be viewed like the wings of an airplane. One without the other is worthless. When working together, great things can happen. Bottom-line business improvements for the organization like higher growth, increased efficiencies, and improved strategic alliance relationships all become possible. These all require action.

However, there are common mistakes that many right-thinking managers make when they claim "It happened on my watch." If not avoided, these mistakes can damage, often seriously, the ability of a leader to be successful. The next chapter will lay those out.

Chapter 3

The Great Accountability Mistakes

Somebody does somethin' stupid, that's human. They don't stop when they see it's wrong, that's a fool.
Elvis Presley

ACCOUNTABILITY MEANS that someone in charge is taking responsibility for a particular outcome or result. "It happened on my watch." It forces action.

The responsibility component takes over when a person claiming accountability takes viable, coherent steps to fix whatever caused the problem in the first place.

If little or no tangible action is taken, then there is no real accountability and the blame game will usually take over.

If action is commenced, then it needs to be done in the right way. Managing by accountability demands it. Doing so allows those who lead to maintain *and* build their credibility in the eyes of their subordinates and superiors while increasing their achievement as managers.

Right vs. Wrong Action

It may be disheartening to say, but merely trying to do something for the right reasons or to demonstrate leadership is still not enough to successfully manage by accountability. The actions that are executed as part of the responsibility component must be the right ones. A bad plan, regardless how well-intentioned, is still a bad plan and will inevitably render bad results. Conversely, a solid, well-thought-out plan based on sound principles will go a long way to achieving beneficial results.

For those of you old enough to remember, the aftermath of the 1979 Three Mile Island crisis provides an example of lousy planning and even worse execution in a situation where management by accountability was sorely lacking. Before the incident at the Pennsylvania nuclear power plant on the Susquehanna River, most people had never heard of the place. When the initial information from the accident in the Unit 2 reactor at the plant began to leak out, it was sketchy and contradictory.

The utility company that ran the plant said the situation was manageable. But officials from the mayor's office to the Oval Office worried about possible complications that would shower radioactivity on the small communities around Three Mile Island—or perhaps even farther. Government engineers feared that the reactor's nuclear fuel would melt out of its thick steel and cement encasement, or that a hydrogen gas bubble in the core would explode.

In Harrisburg, less than ten miles away, the state's new governor struggled with conflicting advice on whether to begin an evacuation that might affect more than 600,000 people. In Washington, 100 miles south, federal regulators anxiously sought reliable information to guide local authorities and the president, former nuclear engineer Jimmy Carter. Sounds a lot like the response to Hurricane Katrina, no?

Revelations during the decade-long cleanup of the crippled reactor showed that its core was more seriously damaged than originally suspected. But scientists still disagree on whether the radiation vented during the event was enough to affect the health of those who lived near the plant.

Although the crisis was the result of equipment and operator failure, reluctance by officials to treat the situation seriously from the onset and from an accountability point of view exacerbated the emergency. The little information released was sketchy and inaccurate. People were angry and frightened. The media had a field day.

Another example of lack of a solid accountability-based plan occurred when Perrier Group of America, Inc. announced a highly embarrassing product recall on February 9, 1990. The recall came in response to a report released by North Carolina regulators that stated Perrier's high-priced bottled water was contaminated with benzene, a poisonous liquid shown to cause cancer in laboratory animals. Even though the U.S. Food and Drug Administration said that the benzene levels did not pose "a significant short-term health risk," Perrier's management requested the removal of the product from supermarkets and restaurants in the United States and Canada. A good first step on the road to managing by accountability.

However, a Perrier official stated at the time that the company believed the contamination could be traced to an employee's mistaken use of a fluid containing benzene to clean the machinery on the bottling line that fills bottles for the North American market. Initially, the recall affected only the United States and Canada—an inventory of some seventy million bottles. Soon it was made worldwide when Dutch and Danish officials also found benzene in some Perrier bottles.

The incident turned into a disaster for the company, in large part because the company's leaders were ducking accountability.

After traces of benzene were found in bottles in other parts of the world, company officials altered their original explanation. Benzene, they now said, is naturally present in carbon dioxide (the gas that makes Perrier bubbly) and is normally filtered out before the water is bottled.

For unknown reasons workers had inexplicably failed to change the filters. Meanwhile, Perrier still insisted that its famous spring in Vergeze, France, was unpolluted. These inconsistent statements and lack of accountability further raised consumers' suspicions.

The big question was what long-term effects the contamination incident would have on Perrier, which had positioned itself as a naturally pure bottled water brand. The strong underpinning for the success of bottled waters was their perceived safety compared to ordinary tap water.

In 1989 Perrier was the leading imported water, holding about 6 percent of the U.S. bottled water segment. But the success brought intense competition from other bottled water brands in the 1990s. While the total category was growing at about 10 percent annually, Perrier's growth slowed to about 5 percent per year.

In an effort to regain market share lost during the months-long recall, Perrier spent $25 million in a U.S. advertising campaign. The message was, "Perrier: Worth Waiting For." However, it seemed that consumers began to believe that any bottled water would do. Exacerbating the problem was the FDA's decision to make Perrier drop the words "Naturally Sparkling" from its label since its investigators had discovered that Perrier artificially carbonates its water after taking it out of the ground. Again, company officials were concerned about what beliefs consumers were forming about the brand.

By 1995, Perrier sales had fallen to one-half their 1989 peak. The company had to mount a comeback strategy. While attempting to regain share for the Perrier brand through new distribution channels, the company began to invest in other brands that did not have the Perrier name attached to them. Despite the company's efforts to regain sales, the brand is still not among the best-selling bottled waters in the United States. The question remains up till today: For how long will the memory of the benzene incident and the lack of accountability forever tarnish the Perrier brand name?

Figuring It Out

In 1982, Johnson & Johnson's Tylenol medication commanded 35 percent of the U.S. over-the-counter analgesic market— representing something like 15 percent of the company's profits.

Unfortunately, at that point one individual succeeded in lacing the drug with cyanide. Seven people died as a result, and a widespread panic ensued about how widespread the contamination might be. By the end of the episode, everyone knew that Tylenol was associated with the scare. Johnson & Johnson management did very little to alleviate the concerns of the public and paid for it. Accountability was nowhere to be seen. The company's market value fell by $1 billion as a result.

Those in charge at Johnson & Johnson got a second chance to set things right when the same situation happened in 1986. The company demonstrated that it had learned its lessons well. It acted quickly—ordering that Tylenol should be recalled from every outlet—not just those in the state where it had been tampered with. Not only that, but the company decided the product would not be reestablished on the shelves until something had been done to provide better product protection.

As a result, Johnson & Johnson developed the tamperproof packaging that would make it much more difficult for a similar incident to occur in future. The cost was a high one. In addition to the impact on the company's share price when the crisis first hit, the lost production and destroyed goods as a result of the recall were considerable.

However, the company won praise for its quick and appropriate action and accountability-based approach. Having sidestepped the position others have found themselves in—of having been slow to act as accountable in the face of consumer concern—they achieved the status of consumer champion through managing by accountability.

Within five months of the disaster, the company had recovered 70 percent of its market share for the drug—and the fact this went on to improve over time showed that the company had succeeded in preserving the long-term value of the brand. In fact, there is some evidence that it was rewarded by consumers who were so reassured by the steps taken that they switched from other painkillers to Tylenol.

They acted quickly, with complete openness about what had happened, and immediately sought to remove any source of danger based on the worst-case scenario—not waiting for evidence to see whether the contamination might be more widespread.

Having acted quickly, they then sought to ensure that measures were taken which would prevent as far as possible a recurrence of the problem. They showed themselves to be prepared to bear the short-term cost in the name of consumer safety—and accountability. That more than anything else established a basis for the trust with their customers, which lasts until today.

The Great Accountability Mistakes

Clearly, people in positions of responsibility should be held to account for what they do. But in many cases, the accountability that is delivered is far short of what is truly needed—for whatever reason. This can be at least partially be attributed to what I label as The Great Accountability Mistakes.

We Set Our Personal Expectations Way Too Low

Accountability is a relationship based on the obligation to demonstrate and take responsibility for performance in light of agreed expectations. It starts not from without but from within. Fundamental to this is the setting of high personal expectations. Many managers expect themselves to perform at the level they think their boss or subordinates want from them. It is very dangerous stuff to assume that their interest and expectations are best for you. They may be. But they also may not.

We Fail to Live the Integrity Imperative

How many business leaders believe they have learnt the lessons taught by Enron? What if I told you that the U.S. Securities and Exchange Commission (SEC) currently receives some 40,000 whistle-blowing reports every month—compared to 6,400 per month the year Enron imploded? Would it make you wonder whether business leaders should take a second look at accountability and the integrity it demands?

We have been misguided into believing that mandated accountability somehow, someway equates to ethics, and that if you have solid corporate governance policies, the ability of the organization and, by association, the people who work in it can be labeled as accountable and sound. Managing successfully by accountability is rooted in a high level of personal integrity, and nothing can replace it.

We Treat Accountability as a Noun, Rather a Verb

If somebody screws up, they will often wrap themselves in the coat of accountability, say something like "Trust me, everything will be fine," and then disappear. This is not managing by accountability.

To avoid the horrors of the blame game, it is incumbent for those who manage by accountability to ensure that term is treated as a verb, not a noun. Action must follow. But in a lot of cases the only output is rhetoric, obfuscation, and little else. . . .

We Fail to See How Change and Conflict Are Directly Tied to Accountability

In today's touchy/feely world, conflict is often held as the worst possible outcome of any situation. In many organizations, if someone simply raises their voice in a meeting—regardless what is said and regardless what spurned it—word about the "incident" spreads like wildfire:

> "Did you hear that Dave got loud at the Tuesday morning meeting?"

> "Yea, can you believe it?"

> "I'll make sure to stay away from him so he doesn't yell at me either."

Change, like leadership, is not always full of glory and pats on the back. It can be ugly, painful, and fraught with conflict. However, if we are to manage by accountability, we need to embrace the short-term sacrifice that change and conflict will inevitably bring—rather than run away from it.

We Don't Help Others Around Us to Develop Personal Accountability

In the world of teams, no manager can be an island. To view ourselves as a singular entity in a universe of strategic alliances, collaborations, and partnerships is short-sighted and detrimental.

We have to work with others. To enhance the effectiveness of our ability to lead, that means helping out others when it comes to their ability to manage by accountability.

Each of these mistakes can torpedo the correct-thinking manager who has chosen accountability as their path. The next chapters will glare through the looking glass on each of these mistakes and turn them on their heads to see clearly the benefits of doing things the right ways. At the end, results, integrity, and effectiveness will become possible for managers as they seek to lead via accountability.

Chapter 4

Set Your Personal
Expectations Higher Than
Those Around You

*It is easy to fool yourself. It is possible to fool the people you work for. It is
more difficult to fool the people you work with. But it is almost
impossible to fool the people who work under you.*
Harry B. Thayer

SAM WALTON ONCE OBSERVED that "high expectations are
the key to everything." To be effective as a manager who adheres
to high standards of personal accountability, it is imperative that
you set your personal expectations higher than those around you
do. In other words, you should expect more from yourself than
your boss or colleagues or subordinates do.

I work in a business that runs 24×7. We have the luxury of
evaluating ourselves every morning. We always tend to focus on
the areas of opportunity, otherwise known as mistakes or miscues.
It is very easy in any position of leadership to fall into the trap of
worrying more about what others think about our performance
than how we measure up to our own standards of performance.

When you wake up every morning in the "how am I going to
explain this to my boss or my subordinates" syndrome, life is not

pleasant. The worst part is, your people see right through this. Instead of a leader, you are a mouthpiece or a puppet or the paper tiger we talked about earlier.

I am convinced that this is one of the major drivers in credibility. People want to have a leader who is confident. One cannot exude confidence if he or she is worried about someone else's expectations. Nor can one truly hold oneself to a high standard of accountability.

There have been so many times that I have heard people say, "Don't do that again because I'll catch hell from my boss!" The best managers are those who led and managed in such a manner that you never saw any evidence that they even had a boss. They were their own boss. They worried about their own high exacting standards and expectations. Standards and expectations that were higher than anyone else's.

They were concerned and even upset if the results were not acceptable, not because of what others would think, but because of what they felt and thought about it. Those leaders gained the respect of their employees. The ones who wore somebody else's expectations on their sleeve did not.

Managers who do not have high expectations and bounce back and forth based on other's reaction are unpredictable. This makes them very difficult to work for. They have great difficulty in making decisions. All of us have, either at one time or another, known someone like this. Seeing these kinds of people in action makes us feel sorry for them. Sympathy does not, however, create respect and credibility.

Probably most of us have had a boss at one time or another who had to pass bad news by blaming on the "higher-ups." "I didn't want to make these cuts but headquarters made me." "I wanted to give you a higher annual performance evaluation, but my boss made me lower it." "I know that no one wants to work forced overtime, but you know what corporate would say if we didn't get this shipment out." All the blame game!

Those who manage by accountability must have high standards and expectations. They have to be able to tell the truth, most important, when the truth may be bad news.

In our company, our field General Managers pride themselves in saying to their people, "Don't look any further up the ladder than me. I am headquarters as far as you are concerned. I have ownership in the decision-making process and I hold myself accountable for the outcomes. I am headquarters."

Water-cooler talk like "I heard his boss made him do it" is not a complement to someone in charge. With someone who manages by accountability, you never know what their superior said. You don't even care. Managers who set high expectations are known to their people as "take charge" leaders. They breed integrity and credibility. And they are great. As Wayne Gretzky used to say, "I skate to where the puck is going to be, not where it is."

What Are Expectations?

Among the most powerful forces we experience in life are expectations. Some expectations come from other people. Parents, spouses, peers, superiors, subordinates, friends, children, neighbors, customers, and plenty of others all have their expectations of us. They expect certain things regarding our speech, our behavior, and our character. Often, the most influential expectations are the ones that go unstated. And the source of some expectations may be hard to define. We allow our lives to be determined by a powerful yet indefinite group we call "they." "They" expect this or that of me, and I feel compelled to satisfy them.

Other expectations come more clearly from within us. We accept certain norms, and expect to follow them. We prize certain goals, and expect to realize them. These internal expectations make their presence known. When they conflict with each other, then we feel the pain of division and confusion until we choose between them.

Some expectations are unjust, whether they come from inside or outside. They demand that we do what we cannot or should not do. What they ask exceeds our ability or does violence to our identity. There are other expectations that are just. They call on us to do what we can or what we need to do. They show us our responsibility to others. They contribute to the establishment of our true identity.

Expectations seem intricately tied to what philosophers have called "virtue." One general and traditional definition of "virtue" is a habit that enables one to do something good easily. This very general definition is encapsulated in the old saying "practice makes perfect." Practice over time creates a habit, an abiding ability, and a skill that enables us to do something with ease. If I pick up a knife and a piece of wood and try to carve something, or even just try to whittle the wood, I will gouge it and ruin it quickly, because I have no practice in carving wood. I have not practiced whittling or carving and I have no ability or skill.

If, however, I spent hours a day learning to whittle or carve, I might well become skilled. I would have acquired the "virtue" of a carver. So too with piano playing or speaking French or dealing with customer service. Of course some people seem to have a natural ability or inclination toward various activities of soul, mind, or body: there are natural athletes, people with seemingly innate musicality or intellectual genius or a gift for languages. But without denying innate dispositions, most activities can be cultivated by practice and habit so that we can acquire the virtue to perform them more easily than we would if we did not practice.

Usually, however, we use the word *virtue* in everyday speech in a different sense. *Virtue* usually implies a moral quality. We may begin with our general definition of virtue (a habit that enables one to do something well with ease), and then apply it to moral matters in recognition of this everyday sense of the word. A moral virtue is a habit of soul that enables one to do moral good and to avoid wrong easily in some respect. For instance, the virtue of honesty in money matters means a habit of respecting the property of others which makes it easy for me to return money belonging to someone else that I have found or easy for me not to surrender to a temptation to steal. In this case we have taken the general idea of a virtue and applied it specifically to a moral matter, to doing moral good and avoiding evil.

The matter of habit, of acquiring a skill or ability or tendency through repetition or custom or gradual development or practice, remains. Virtue at its core is true understanding of one's own abilities when setting expectations. It's a funny thing about life; if you refuse to accept anything but the best, you very often get it. The world is full of abundance and opportunity, but far too many people come to the fountain of life with a sieve instead of a tank car . . . a teaspoon instead of a steam shovel. They expect little and as a result they get little.

Seeing the Expectations Before They Materialize

To be someone who manages by accountability, the future belongs to those who see possibilities before they become obvious. There are risks and costs to a program of action and setting your expectations higher than those of the individuals around you. But they are far less than the long-range risks and costs of comfortable inactions. Great leaders are those who get up and look for circumstances they want, and if they can't find them, they make them. This is done through the development of habits.

Since the time of Aristotle at least, writers interested in moral matters have noted the importance of habit in developing character and setting one's expectations That is, they note the importance of developing habits that dispose children, and then adults, to expect to do the right thing. Custom becomes second nature. Habits incline us one way or the other. These habitual inclinations, if they dispose us toward doing good, are virtues. If they dispose us toward doing evil, they are vices.

A virtue doesn't destroy free will. A truthful person, for instance, is someone who is accustomed to telling the truth, even when doing so is embarrassing or personally costly. This benchmarks their expectation of themselves when it comes to truthfulness. Such a person, however, may be tempted to lie and may actually do so. The virtue of truthfulness makes it easier for the person to resist the temptation; at least if he tells a lie it will be against his inclination and will probably prick his conscience. Virtues and vices are habits and dispositions, which make something easier or harder, but not inevitable. The sum of our habits of soul, our virtues and vices, is our character. The idea that character and virtue, which determine our expectations, are essentially private and not of concern in a setting like business is short-sighted and dangerous in the extreme. Tyco, Enron, Adelphia, Global Crossing, et al. show us what omitting character and virtue and having no valid expectations except greed can do.

Getting What You Expect

You often get what you expect. As a manager, this is a very powerful reality, which you can harness to work for you, or you can let it control performance in a negative way. It is your job to set and use expectations in a manner that supports and enhances performance. The theory that expectations affect performance is known as the Pygmalion Principle. Its name is derived from a Greek myth in which a sculptor named Pygmalion sculpted a statue of a woman, and fell in love with it.

His love was so strong that it transformed the statue into a real woman. It is this transformative effect resulting from expectations which is the basis of the Pygmalion Principle. Research in the field of education has supported the theory by demonstrating that students who the teacher believed were smarter than the rest of the group (when they were actually randomly chosen) performed substantially better than those believed to be "average." In these experiments, the only difference between the students who performed best and the rest of the group was the teacher's expectations. As a manager, you also have the power to influence employee's performance through the expectations you set on yourself.

Setting Your Expectations

Here are seven keys that will help you set the kinds of expectations that will enable you to effectively manage by accountability.

Have Clear Expectations

Effective managers are not vague about the things that they want to do. They are definite about their aims and responsibilities. Be as specific as possible when setting goals.

Commit Wholeheartedly to Fulfilling Your Expectations

Managing by accountability implies being prepared to do what it takes to get the job done. This means that they must press on through discouragement, stand firm in trials, and learn how to handle disappointment and stay faithful when tempted to drift or stray.

Ensure That the Expectation Is Realistic for You

Can you see yourself achieving it? Expectations must be realistic and down-to-earth too. I know that faith can move mountains and all things are possible for those who believe. But I could never see myself beating Tiger Woods at this year's U.S. Open. No matter how much faith I have, the expectation is not viable. Occasionally, we are all prone to set impractical expectations. We must be practical and see ourselves achieving the goals that we set.

Write Down Your Expectations

Those which are written down are over twenty times more likely to be achieved than goals not made explicit. Write down the things that will prevent you from achieving your expectations also. This keeps us vigilant and prompts us to take evasive action when our expectations are threatened. Fear, doubt, and uncertainty are just some examples of what might stop leaders from achieving their goals. But if we remind ourselves of these pitfalls, we will more than likely take steps to steer clear of them or deal firmly with them when they arise. Is there anything in your life that could stop you achieving the things that you have set out to do? If so deal with the foes now. Ask yourself "What effect will achieving this expectation have on me?" If you were to reach a goal of getting a new job promotion or starting up a relationship, what effect is it going to have on you?

Determine How You Will Know When You've Achieved Your Expectations

Do you know when your goals have been reached? They are not endless projects and responsibilities. We have to identify what success looks like. We have to acknowledge when our job's done and realize when our tasks are completed. We must know when our dreams come true and see when our vision is fulfilled.

When setting their expectations, those who manage by accountability should always ask, "Is this thing right for me? Is the timing right for doing this project?" Remember too that different goals have different gestation periods. A chicken egg takes twenty-one days to break into life, a human embryo takes nine months, and an elephant takes two years. Expectations are like that. Some are accomplished quickly, some take many years.

Chapter 5

Live the Integrity Imperative

The question for each man to settle is not what he would do if he had the means, time, influence and educational advantages, but what he will do with the things he has.
Hamilton Wright Mabee

RIGHT AFTER TAKING the helm of our company, Matt Rose, our current CEO, inherited a crisis that threatened to tear apart the very fabric of the organization. It involved charges of genetic manipulation, threats of massive lawsuits, and a visit by *60 Minutes*. Not a good combination, to say the least.

Senior management had learned that some frontline workers in Nebraska were in the process of initiating lawsuits against the company because they claimed the railroad had been doing some genetic testing on them without their knowledge. The first inclination was to deny the charges and say they were not a possibility. Matt, however, decided to fully explore the situation before the company made any further comments or took action.

While, under Matt's direction, we were trying to get to the bottom of what had actually happened, *60 Minutes* got fired up about the possibility of a big, bad corporate giant taking advantage of its workers. And the ball started rolling. . . .

A typical *60 Minutes* story can take upwards of six months from the time production starts until it is aired. This case was no exception. At the outset, we were originally contacted by their producers and we told them we had no comment until a determination could be made as to what took place. Undaunted, *60 Minutes* moved forward and interviewed all of the employees, their lawyers, and seemingly anyone else who had it in for the company.

As time wore on, it was discovered that in fact some genetic testing had taken place by some managers who were hoping to reduce back injuries in our employees—a common problem many of our folks experience due to the rigors of their jobs. They were trying to do the right thing, but were going about it in the wrong way.

When Matt learned of this, he immediately put an action plan in place that dealt with the errant managers and made restitution with the wronged workers. He also wrote a letter to *60 Minutes* saying the company and, specifically himself, were accountable for what had happened and detailed the responsible action that had been taken to solve the problem once and for all.

There was no cover-up. There was nothing done to cause further damage to the workers who made the charges. There was no blame game. In short, it wasn't news. Nevertheless, *60 Minutes* ran the story. Conversely, in the Enron, Tyco, and WorldCom cases, which were unfolding around the same time, no one at the highest levels of those companies ever admitted anything wrong was ever done.

Warren Buffett said it correctly when he observed that to be folks who manage by accountability, managers don't need independent directors, oversight committees, or auditors absolutely free of conflicts of interest to keep an eye on them. They need to quit talking about the bad apples and reflect instead on their own behavior. They simply need to do what's right.[1]

After I observed Matt's behavior in this difficult time as a new CEO, and saw that he managed by accountability, I was certain that he was someone I could work for.

Integrity Means Action

It's what we do that counts. Not what we don't do. Or what we intend to do. Taking action and making decisions is an open window into what we are about both as people and as leaders. Making decisions defines our value and benchmarks our credibility.

"Pleasers" and "Yes Men"

Throughout my career, I have made every effort never to be a pleaser or a "yes man." These are kinds of managers that can destroy an organization. How many times do managers try to read the tea leaves and guess where the popular opinions are. Often these leaders simply don't know any better: they don't know how to determine the right course for themselves, so they take polls to see whether the winds of popular opinion are blowing on a particular day and simply give the people what they want. The problem is that predicting the direction of the majority is just as difficult as predicting the winds of weather. And, it has no basis in accountable behavior.

There is always a strong temptation for leaders to please people.... Why? To be popular, to not make enemies, to not seem hateful and unloving, so people won't get mad at them, to keep the peace and to keep their job. ... And when we run around trying to please people, we become like the guy spinning plates at the circus.

When I was brand new at my current company, I had an initial meeting with a boss a few levels above me: an unflappable, grandfatherly gentleman who was known throughout the industry as a leader of integrity and action. During our conversation, I made a flippant comment, something like "I just want to please you."

He immediately turned beet red. He darted back, "If you think your role here is to please me, you couldn't be farther from the truth. You are here to do your job!"

Although "Yes men" are common everywhere and can hurt things by agreeing with everything you say, pleasers are the worst. Pleasers are the enemy. They go out of their way to hide problems and obfuscate the truth. And, by not disclosing the truth, they can ruin the whole year or your career.

Living the integrity imperative means being able to deliver the bad news. Whether your boss or your subordinates, if they have to hear bad news from someone else, your credibility as a manager is shot. Managing by accountability means the ability to deliver the bad news on time and without candy coating. This will raise the respect level for you from both your boss and subordinates.

Moreover, many times, those above and below you in the organizational structure will already know the bad news before you do. Trying to hide or bury or parse out the truth can make you look foolish and weak.

An ancient Persian proverb offers the following excellent advice on leaders who manage by accountability and action.

> He who knows not, and knows not that he knows not is a fool—shun him.
>
> He who knows not, and knows that he knows not is a child—teach him.
>
> He who knows, and knows not that he knows is asleep—wake him.
>
> He who knows, and knows that he knows is wise—follow him.

An influential person will choose accountability. To be responsible to others and themselves; to allow others to call themselves to account. An unaccountable person, on the other hand, will answer to no one except the popular whims of the moment. At its core, personal accountability is about character. It welcomes the integrity imperative and embraces it. It is the direct opposite of management by public opinion poll or by "yes men" and pleasers.

Harry Truman hit it square on the head when he observed, "I wonder how far Moses would have gone if he had taken a poll in the Egyptian desert? How far would the Reformation have gone if Martin Luther had taken a poll? It isn't the popular opinion of the moment that counts. It is right and wrong and leadership—men with fortitude, honesty, and a belief in the right—that makes epochs in the history of the world."

Integrity Is More Than the Public View

To make the point that integrity is more than what we do in public, a friend of mine takes out a $20 bill and asks his employees, "Who would like this $20 bill?" Then he crumples it up, steps on it, rolls it around, and then holds it up again and asks, "Who still wants this $20 bill?"

The value remains no matter what the item looks like on the outside—no matter how scarred, bruised, or beaten, the value is still the same. That is integrity.

So fearful were the ancient Chinese of their enemies on the north that they built the Great Wall, one of the Seven Wonders of the Ancient World. It was so high they knew no one could climb over it, and so thick that nothing could break it down. Then they settled back to enjoy their security.

But during the first one hundred years of the wall's existence, China was invaded three times—from the north! Not once did the enemy break down the wall or climb over its top. Each time they bribed a gatekeeper and marched right through the gates. The Chinese were so busy relying on the walls of stone that they forgot to teach integrity to their children. To lead effectively, the inside needs to match up with the outside persona.

Some time ago, I heard about a fellow in Cleveland who went into a fried-chicken franchise to get some chicken for himself and the young lady with him. She waited in the car while he went in to pick up the chicken. Inadvertently, the manager of the store handed the guy the box in which he had placed the financial proceeds of the day instead of the box of chicken. You see, he was going to make a deposit and had camouflaged it by putting the money in a fried-chicken box. The fellow took his box, went back to the car, and the two of them drove away.

When they got to the park for their picnic and opened the box, they discovered they had a box full of money. The guy realized there must have been a mistake, so he got back in his car and returned to the place and gave the money back to the manager. Well, the manager was elated!

He was so pleased that he told the young man, "Stick around, I want to call the newspaper and have them take your picture. You're the honest guy in town."

"Oh, no, don't do that!" said the fellow. "Why not?" asked the manager. "Well," he said, "You see, I'm married, and the woman I'm with right now is not my wife."

On the surface of life, it is a lot easier to demonstrate integrity. We return money that's not ours. We pay our bills on time. We work hard at our jobs. We volunteer at church. But if someone were to write a story about your life, about the things nobody else knows, would we really want him or her to write everything?

Integrity—Inside and Out—in Action

Day after day, Goliath paraded along the slopes of the Valley of Elah threatening and blaspheming the armies of Israel. And they were all afraid of him. Goliath had a basic strategy. INTIMIDA-TION! And it worked! No one would fight him. Every morning and every evening for 40 days Goliath came out to taunt his enemies.

On the other side, Saul and the men of Israel were gathered and camped in the valley of Elah, and drew up in battle array to encounter the Philistines. The Philistines stood on the mountain on one side, while Israel stood on the mountain on the other side, with the valley between them.

Goliath was six cubits in height (9 feet 9 inches tall). He had a bronze helmet on his head, and he was clothed with scale-armor that weighed five thousand shekels of bronze. The weight of five thousand shekels weight equals 125 pounds!

He also had bronze greaves on his legs and a bronze javelin slung between his shoulders. The shaft of his spear was like a weaver's beam, and the head of his spear weighed six hundred shekels of iron (15 pounds); his shield-carrier also walked before him.

He stood and shouted to the ranks of Israel and said to them, "Why do you come out to draw up in battle array? Am I not the Philistine and you servants of Saul? Choose a man for yourselves and let him come down to me."

"If he is able to fight with me and kill me, then we will become your servants; but if I prevail against him and kill him, then you shall become our servants and serve us."

Again the Philistine said, "I defy the ranks of Israel this day; give me a man that we may fight together."

The Philistines proposed a battle in which two representative champions from Israel and Philistia would duel it out, a not uncommon method of limiting war in the ancient world. It minimized bloodshed and made life a whole lot easier for everybody, that is, if your champion won.

However, the Israelites had no one who could compete with Goliath. When Saul and all Israel heard these words of the Philistine, they were dismayed and greatly afraid. And it went on and on and on for 40 days. . . .

The dawn of the 41st day though was the beginning of the end for Goliath. There was a young shepherd boy sent on an errand by his father that took him into the vicinity where this insulting

Goliath was parading his strength. David stopped and stared in disbelief when Goliath pulled this shenanigan that day.

Something happened within David at that moment. "No giant should ever be able to intimidate anyone this way. He's going down."

Then Saul clothed David with his garments and put a bronze helmet on his head, and he clothed him with armor. David girded his sword over his armor and tried to walk, for he had not tested them. So David said to Saul, "I cannot go with these, for I have not tested them." And David took them off. He took his stick in his hand and chose for himself five smooth stones from the brook, and put them in the shepherd's bag that he had, even in his pouch, and his sling was in his hand.

Then the Philistine came on and approached David, with the shield-bearer in front of him. When the Philistine looked and saw David, he disdained him; for he was but a youth, and ruddy, with a handsome appearance. Goliath has got to be thinking, "They have sent me a red-headed pretty-boy. I'm insulted by that."

The Philistine said to David, "Am I a dog, that you come to me with sticks?" And added, "Come to me, and I will give your flesh to the birds of the sky and the beasts of the field."

Then it happened when the Philistine rose and came and drew near to meet David that David ran quickly toward the battle line to meet the Philistine.

You know the outcome. "Thus David prevailed over the Philistine with a sling and a stone, and he struck the Philistine and killed him; but there was no sword in David's hand."

Then David ran and stood over the Philistine and took his sword and drew it out of its sheath and killed him, and cut off his head with it. (If the stone merely knocked him out as some suggest, then this would finish the job for sure.) When the Philistines saw that their champion was dead, they fled.

David was a man of integrity. When a person sees a great injustice, a great need, and a great leadership vacuum, they rise up and say, "Things must be different and I will be a difference-maker." David's story teaches us that an inspired person of integrity can beat a mighty military warrior with but the tools of a shepherd and a heart of integrity.

the words *ne plus ultra* underneath. However, the lion is eating the first word *ne*. All that can be read is "more beyond." This was Columbus's greatest legacy—he proved that there was more beyond—because he acted.

Learning from Ants

Have you ever heard of a myrmecologist? No, it's not a person who studies "murmuring." Myrmecology is the study of ants. I don't know about devoting one's whole life to studying the little things, but I do know that much of success as a manager has a lot to do with the way ants operate.

It Is the Little Things That Matter

There are over 10,000 different species of ants. They are able to lift twenty times their own body weight. This means that if I had their strength I could lift approximately 4,000 lbs. Ants have been found to build structures 500 times their own height. The brain of one ant has 250,000 cells whereas the human brain has 10 billion cells

Ants also have two stomachs—one for storing up food to share with others later, and one for itself. The life expectancy of an ant is 45–60 days. Yet these tiny creatures accomplish much in a very short life-span. And they can teach a whole lot about how to treat accountability as a noun rather than a verb.

Some years ago a young man approached the foreman of a logging crew and asked for a job. "That depends," replied the foreman. "Let's see you fell this tree." The young man stepped forward and skillfully felled a great tree. Impressed, the foreman exclaimed, "Great! You can start Monday!"

Monday, Tuesday, Wednesday, Thursday rolled by, and Thursday afternoon the foreman approached the young man and said, "You can pick up your paycheck on the way out today."

Startled, he replied, "I thought you paid on Friday." "Normally we do," answered the foreman, "but we're letting you go today because you've fallen behind. Our daily felling charts show that you've dropped from first place on Monday to last on Wednesday."

"But I'm a hard worker," the young man objected. "I arrive first, leave last, and even have worked through my coffee breaks!"

The foreman, sensing the boy's shock, thought for a minute and then asked, "Have you been sharpening your ax?"

The young man replied, "I've been working too hard to take the time."

To Perform with a High Degree of Accountability, There Must Be a Plan—but Don't Plan Too Much!

At first glance at an anthill, you just see a lot of activity. Ants running around everywhere—but they have a plan. I believe that there are a lot of managers in companies who are active and whose departments are filled with programs, committees, and red tape—but they have no plan. They have no vision for the future. They have little if any idea as to what their function is, and which way they are going. Accountable managers must have a vision. They must be as wise as ants. They must make all that they do count for the betterment of the organization.

There is an amusing story from General Stonewall Jackson's famous valley campaign during the Civil War that illustrates this. Jackson's army found itself on one side of a river when it needed to be on the other side. After telling his engineers to plan and build a bridge so the army could cross, he called his wagon master in to tell him that it was urgent the wagon train cross the river as soon as possible. The wagon master started gathering all the logs, rocks, and fence rails he could find and built a bridge. Long before daylight General Jackson was told by his wagon master all the wagons and artillery had crossed the river. General Jackson asked where are the engineers and what are they doing? The wagon master's only reply was that they were in their tent drawing up plans for a bridge.

To Perform with Efficiency There Must Be Participation from Others

Take a look at an anthill and you don't see ants just sitting around or standing around doing nothing. Every one of those ants has a job, and no one has to tell them what it is. And no one has to push them to do it. Wouldn't you like your office to work like that?

Human beings seem to be the only creatures who do things half-way; throw things together at the last moment; put little, if any, time or planning into their efforts. We show up at the last minute unprepared. If ants ran their hills like a lot of people run their businesses, the species would be dead within a year. As Abraham Lincoln observed, "You can't escape the responsibility of tomorrow by evading it today."

Ants work together in harmony. You know how they're able to do it? Each ant is accountable to itself more than any other ant. And they're so busy doing what they're supposed to do that they don't have time to fight among themselves!

Preparedness Is Vital

Ants don't know the meaning of procrastination. They don't wait till the weather turns cold before they are preparing. They gather food while it is still warm and take it into their colony. Many of those who work hard all day will never eat of the food they are preparing because they will die before cold weather. But they want to make certain that their families are taken care of.

The Relationship of Confidence and Action

Confidence

If there is one quality we should have that'll make us successful in taking action, it is confidence. What are the benefits of having confidence? The Gallup organization regularly takes national surveys to study the impact of self-esteem and confidence on people. The results are always that people with a high level of self-confidence are more successful, are more satisfied with their lives, are more willing to help others in need, are physically healthier, hold themselves to higher moral and ethical standards, and are more likely to assume leadership.

John Maxwell says that confidence stabilizes you and at the same stretches you. Confidence gives you a foundation to build upon and it frees you up to take risks. Insecure people seldom stretch because they are not confident enough to live life on the edge. Jim Loehr said, "With confidence, you can reach truly amazing heights; without confidence, even the simplest accomplishments are beyond your grasp."

Confidence and Accountability in Action

Another benefit of having confidence in yourself and the actions you take is that it brings comfort to others. Imagine having a surgery. You're nervous. Before the surgery, your doctor comes into the room to meet you and talk to you. And he is sort of pale and his hands are sweaty, and he's shaking nervously and he says to you, "I don't know how this surgery's going to go, but I'll do my best and feel around in there and see what I can find." A doctor needs to be confident so that his patients will be comfortable. Can you imagine an airline pilot coming over the intercom with a quiver in his voice saying, "I hope we'll be able to land this baby in

Dallas. Keep your fingers crossed." A pilot needs to be confident in his actions so that people on the plane feel confident.

If you've ever been to the Kennedy Space Center, you'll probably agree that one of the highlights of the spectacular tour is the restored Saturn V rocket. Millions of people held their breath while a single man stepped onto the moon's surface. For those who remember, the event remains in their minds just as those footprints remain in the lunar soil. At Kennedy Space Center, in a spacious facility featuring a massive, real Saturn V rocket, those moments return spectacularly to life. The Apollo/Saturn V Center is a tribute to the Apollo Astronauts and the machines that got them there—and brought them safely home.

Saturn V was developed to carry the Apollo spacecraft into lunar orbit. At 104 tons, the rocket payload was roughly four times that of the Space Shuttle. In order to launch what at that time would be the largest rocket ever and most complex machine ever built, a special rocket assembly facility and No. 39 launch complex was constructed at the Kennedy Space Center.

At liftoff, the entire launch vehicle (including spacecraft) was 363 ft high; it weighed 6.3 million pounds; and the five Saturn first-stage engines generated 7.7 million pounds of thrust.

The first test launch of the Saturn V took place in November 1967. In December 1968, the third Saturn V to be launched sent Apollo 8 around the Moon. The sixth Saturn V launched on July 20, 1969, propelled Apollo 11 to the Moon for the first successful manned landing on the lunar surface. The Saturn V rocket was used for subsequent Apollo missions to the Moon. With termination of the Apollo program after the Apollo 17 mission, however, three Saturn V rockets out of the total of fifteen produced remained unused.

A good friend of my coauthor is a gentleman named Paul Thomarios, who owns several businesses in the Akron, Ohio, area, including painting, coating, and construction companies.

Paul's father, a Greek immigrant from Asia Minor who was in Seattle when the Nazis conquered his country, moved to Akron with his family following World War II after serving four years with the U.S. Army. His Dad's family painting business prospered over the years and was taken over by Paul in the early 1970s.

In 1996, the Smithsonian Institute invited bids to restore one of the remaining Saturn V rockets for eventual display at the Kennedy Space Center. Paul's company submitted a bid and waited. It was widely known that some of the biggest government contractors had put forward their proposals as well. As the pool of candidates for the job was reduced, Paul's company remained in the running. Finally, "to his shock and delight," Paul was informed that he was one of the last two finalists for the job.

Paul was told that he and the other bidder were to each make a presentation to a group of Smithsonian and NASA employees as well as an undisclosed number of government consultants. Paul traveled to Florida and learned upon his arrival that the other bidder was the formidable Bechtel—a huge multinational conglomerate that does billions of dollars of business a year with the Federal Government.

The meeting was scheduled so that the team from Bechtel— twelve or thirteen in total—would go first. Paul waited alone outside in the lobby. When he was called, he was a bit taken back by the forty-eight people gathered in the room. A soft-spoken man, Paul began to speak about the family values of his company and the abilities of his team. Then he said something that demonstrates how confidence and action are so intertwined:

"If we get this business, I will move down here full-time, along with several of my key employees, until the job is done. You will have us twenty-four hours a day, seven days a week."

The Director of the project thanked Paul and asked him to wait outside in the lobby, along with the entourage from Bechtel. After about fifteen minutes, the Director came out and graciously told the Bechtel guys they could leave. Then he told Paul that it was decided he would get the bid.

The Director told him, "If I give the bid to Bechtel, I know I'll never see those guys again. By giving it to you, I know you will personally be accountable and act accordingly."

The $2.3 million project involved removal of hazardous coatings and reconstruction of the rockets without interruption of public tours or the Space Center's operation, including monthly space shuttle launches. It was completed under an accelerated construction schedule, and with such a high degree of quality that Paul's company—Thomarios®—received a "Best Contractor" award from the Smithsonian Institute.

Chapter 7

Accept Inevitable Change
and Conflict and
Accountability's Role

The greatest separator in our world is action. There are those that do
and those that don't.
John Maxwell

WHO IS REALLY the consistent leader? The person who changes. Since change is the natural law of our being, a leader cannot be consistent if they are stuck in a rut. And how can things really change if no one is ever held to account for their actions? Accountability is fundamental to changing anything that is poorly performing or not working at all. If people know they will be held to account for that which they do, they are much more likely to change.

Without some system of accountability, most people won't change. You (and they) can write plans all day long. But if someone isn't involved in holding you (or them) accountable, it probably won't happen. The old adage "It's not what's expected, but what's inspected, that gets done" still holds true.

So, how are you building accountability into your life? Your organization's? Your employee's performance? Because if there is no accountability, there probably won't be any change. There may be effort, but there won't be significant change.

But here's the problem. Most people don't like change in their lives. One man once wryly observed that the only people who DO like change are "wet babies " . . . and even they aren't too excited about it.

Even the venerable Henry Ford had issues when it came to dealing with the inevitability of change. Back in 1912, Ford Motor Co. had a production manager named William Knudsen—considered one of the best in his field. Knudsen became convinced that the Model T (which had been in production for four years now) had to be updated. But, the only problem was, Henry Ford loved his creation so much it was well known that he opposed changing anything about the car.

According to Robert Lacey, in his best-selling biography, *Ford: The Man and the Machine*, Knudsen thought to convince Ford by building an updated and impressive model to show what could be done with a few changes in color and design.

Ford had just returned from a European vacation, and he went to a Highland Park, Michigan, garage and saw the new design created by Knudsen. On-the-scene mechanics later revealed how Ford responded:

They say that the car was a four-door job, and the top was down, painted gleaming red and built on a new, low slung version of the Model T.

One eyewitness tells how "Ford had his hands in his pockets, and he walked around that car 3 or 4 times. . . . Finally, he got to the left hand side of the car, and he takes his hands out, gets hold of the door, and bang! He ripped the door right off! . . . How the man done it, I don't know! He jumped in there, and bang goes the other door. Bang goes the windshield. He jumps over the back seat and starts pounding on the top. He rips the top with the heel of his shoe. He wrecked the car as much as he could."[1]

Knudsen left for General Motors. Henry Ford nursed along the Model T, but design changes in competitors' models made it more old-fashioned than he would admit. Competitive necessity finally backed him into making the Model A, but his heart was never in it.

Henry Ford was one of the most creative men of his era. And yet even Ford resisted the obvious need for inevitable change.

The Fear of Change and Conflict

Many well-intentioned managers I know who want to manage by accountability live in constant fear that any substantive effort to change and improve will cause tumult and damaging conflict. They are right to be scared. If accountability means the responsibility to act, then action undertaken will lead to some kind of change. And change by its nature causes some degree of upheaval.

However, if we really want to manage by accountability, how is it possible to avoid all that? We can't. Just because something is uncomfortable and causes pain should never serve as an excuse for a leader who is compelled to act.

I realize this puts managers who want to do the right things in a tough spot. They know managing by accountability mandates that changes must be made in order to achieve progress. And they also know it can be very painful and difficult. Conflict will arise from people who perceive any effort to change as threats to their well-being. In this and my other books, I never said being an effective, results-oriented leader was easy and glamorous. It is tough stuff. Not everybody is cut out for it. Overcoming the natural fear of change and conflict is necessary to succeed as a leader.

In my younger days as an upstart manager, I was out on an inspection trip in a major Western city where we had two rail facilities, one right downtown and another just on the edge of town. Our business was large enough only to keep both of the facilities running at half-capacity. When a facility runs at half-capacity, it becomes very difficult to gain a reasonable return on the assets base.

I thought to myself, we should close the facility downtown and move all of the operations to the other facility. This was doable; in fact it would provide tremendous efficiencies for the operation and improve customer service. The risk was that we would have little margin for error. Moreover, I was pushing the existing managers who were very comfortable with what they had. They did not see the need to change. It was a smooth operation that was never in trouble. The management was happy and the employees were happy. Why should they change?

The property in the downtown facility was prime real estate. We could not only make the operation more efficient, but could also sell the valuable land under it for a small fortune. However, what would happen if we closed the yard, consolidated the facilities, sold the expensive land, and operations ultimately suffered? There would be no back-up plan. It was all or nothing.

The only option was to manage the operation so that you did not need a failsafe. The problem was that this group had never done that before. It was like a high-wire act without a net. This change would result in the need for fewer employees. They were not going to like that one bit. There was no doubt that complaints would arise. They would probably reach the general manager's office 500 miles away very quickly.

At the tip of the sword, was the terminal manager, twenty years my senior. He was proud of his accomplishments. He planned to stay right there on that job until he retired. He did not want to do anything to jeopardize his plan. Life was good, he made his numbers, and no one bothered him. Why take a risk?

I had never taken on such a challenge with so many obstacles, barriers, and potential pitfalls. Yet, I could see very clearly the opportunity before me. I knew that it could work. I had almost everything figured right, except the terminal manager.

Not wanting to risk discussing the idea with him, I decided to bring in a study group of time and motion experts to quantify the work events at the facilities to demonstrate that the plan would work. The second day that these clipboard-laden efficiency eggheads showed up, the terminal manager called and asked me to fly out and meet with him. So I did.

"Dave, just level with me, I know that you are trying to prove something. Why don't you just tell me what you are thinking about," he said.

I thought carefully about what I was going to say before I said it. I then explained to him in very careful language what the experts and others thought. Matter-of-factly, he stated, "That's doable." It just about knocked me off my chair.

He added that they'd wanted to do this project for a long while, but had never received backing from senior management to pull it off.

Now they had the backing, and it was their idea, not mine. I was not changing anything, they were. I did not make the change, I facilitated it.

That was twenty years ago. We made the change. It worked. The property we sold to the city is now a major league sports stadium. We hit a home run and I learned a valuable lesson. While most people don't like change, they would rather be the changer than the chang-ee. They like being the changer even more when they have support.

It wasn't until four years ago that I was able to sit in the stadium, enjoy a baseball game with a beer and a hot dog, and think about that whole sequence of events. I had a big smile on my face as I raised my glass in the air in a celebratory toast to everyone who had helped pull it off. What would have happened had fear taken over and nothing had been done. I can't say for sure, but the net result would certainly have been much less in the long run.

To Effectively Lead You Have to Just Get Over It

In the movie *Back to the Future*, Marty McFly goes back in time to the year 1955 to make sure that his mom falls in love with his dad. There's a scene where Marty tries to get his dad to ask her out.

And the dad says, "You mean on a date?"

Marty says, "Yeah."

The timid dad says, "Gee, I don't know, Marty. I mean, what if she says no? What if she laughs at me? I just don't think I can take that kind of a rejection. You know what I mean?"

Marty looks down and says, "Yes. Yes, I know what you mean."

The truth is that we all know what he means. No one likes to be rejected. It hurts. It makes you feel like you're not good enough. That everyone is better than you. That you're a loser.

Some of us have experienced rejection up-close and personal. Maybe you had a boyfriend or girlfriend who didn't want to be with you anymore. Or maybe there was a job that you lost. Or maybe you had a boss who kept yelling, "You'll never amount to anything!"

Whatever it was, at some point in your life, you experienced a painful rejection. And you decided then and there that you didn't want to be hurt like that ever again.

For some people, all that matters is popularity. "What will other people think of me? What if I don't do what he wants me to do? What if he or she rejects me? What if I fail? What if things don't work out?"

The reason why many of us are crippled by a fear is because we care more about what people think than about what is necessary and right to get things done. To achieve great things as a manager, you simply have to get over that. You have to roll up your sleeves and say, "I don't care what these people say about me anymore. The only thing I'm concerned about is what is right for the organization and my people."

We Must Know Where We Are Going and What We Are Going to Do!

This is where integrity really plays a major role in how we lead. It gives us the compass when everything around us is dark and foggy. It lets us know where we are headed.

When he was eighty-eight years old, the late Supreme Court Justice Oliver Wendell Holmes was traveling on a train. The conductor came by and asked for his ticket. Judge Holmes searched his pockets and fumbled through his wallet without success.

The conductor was sympathetic: "Don't worry, Mr. Holmes, the Pennsylvania Railroad will be happy to trust you. When you reach your destination, you will probably find the ticket and you can mail it to us."

The conductor's kindness did not put Justice Holmes at ease. Holmes said, "My dear man, my problem is not where is my ticket? My problem is, I have forgotten where I am going."

Many of us are having the same problem today. We are sold on the ticket, but we aren't clear just where we are going.

You Can't Hide from Conflict

A British friend of mine once told me of a story in the early 1980s of a retired couple who were so alarmed by the threat of nuclear war that they undertook a serious study of all the inhabited places on the globe. Their goal was to determine where in the world would be the place least likely to be affected by a nuclear war—a place of ultimate peace and security. They studied and traveled, traveled and studied. Finally they found the place. And on Christmas they sent a friend a card from their new home—in the Falkland Islands. However, their "paradise" was soon turned into a war zone by Great Britain and Argentina in the conflict, now recorded in history books as the Falklands War.

The civil rights activist James Baldwin is credited with observing, "Most of us are about as eager to be changed as we were to be born, and go through our changes in a similar state of shock."

One of my favorite analogies on the subject of change and its inevitability comes from management consultant Peter Vail. He points out that society is rapidly changing and compares this to living permanently in white water. You have two choices: either jump out of the canoe or grab a paddle. If you have ever rafted, you know that steering a course through white water is not an easy task. Nor is living with constant change. Vail observes that navigating the rapids is hard work: things are only partially under control, yet the effective navigator of the rapids is not behaving randomly or aimlessly. Intelligence, experience, and skill are being exercised, albeit in ways that we hardly know how to perceive, let alone describe. If you understand that responses to change are normal and predictable—and that conflict is predictable—then chances are that change can be managed.[2]

Studies have shown that the most common reaction to change is resistance. I am sure you have experienced this. The reasons why people resist change are many. Chief among them are excessive uncertainty. If we don't know where the next step will lead, we tend to stay put. Our desire for familiar surroundings (or processes) is strong. Change can also cause us to question our competence to continue to do our job or to fear others questioning how we have done that job in the past. Finally, resistance is fueled by the specter of losing control. This is all very natural.

The Misconceptions Surrounding Conflict

Our attitude toward conflict shapes how we as leaders handle conflict. What is your initial attitude toward conflict? Is it dread? Denial? Maybe fear? Perhaps, "What a hassle!" How about procrastination or deflection? ("Let someone else handle it.") Or do you accept conflict as a natural part of life, not preferred, but part of the reality of leadership and choose to use it as a tool for growth and progress? The last response is the wise and healthy response, but also the most difficult.

Misconceptions about conflict do managers a disservice when it comes to seeing the value in conflict and attaining resolution. One misconception is that all conflict is negative. There are many forms of conflict, from Supreme Court issues to scientific debate to methods of child rearing between loving parents that sharpen all of us and develop us as people. Admittedly, there is a difference between disagreement and conflict. It is, however, a fine line and something as subjective as an individual's personality may cause one person to view a situation as a simple disagreement and another to view the same situation as conflict.

Whichever end of the spectrum you are at, and whether or not you perceive it as negative or positive, strongly shapes how you handle it. If you perceive it as negative, you may attempt to do anything to avoid it or get out of it as soon as possible. If you see it as positive, not enjoying it, but embracing the potential for growth, you will have a completely different approach and outcome.

Another misconception is that people are always hurt by conflict. That is not true. It is similar to going to the dentist. I find no joy whatsoever in going to my dentist, but the long-term results are positive and in my best interest. One of the things I thoroughly enjoy is deep political discussion. Not that I'm wise or profound, actually more the opposite, but I am a good student and I love to learn. Tension can mount quickly over political convictions, but as a result of some of the most difficult conversations, I have learned the most. If I had beefed up my defenses, stopped listening, and launched an attack, I may have felt victorious, but I would have learned nothing.

A third misconception is that people are too fragile to handle conflict. Someone once said, "Without conflict, there would be no free market." The business world is packed with conflict and it is something anyone who wants to make an impact must manage.

In fact, conflict has tenable benefits for those who manage by accountability if they look for them. Most important, conflict helps discover the real you and the strength of your character. Most of us will never be tested in as dramatic a way as was the Old Testament character Job. But life has its way of testing us in everyday ways as well. How do you react when someone cuts you off while driving? What about when you receive an angry e-mail from someone? Or a telemarketing call in the middle of dinner? Your response reveals much about the real you. How little or how much it takes to upset you gives great insights to your character. How quickly you pursue positive solutions and forgiveness and how slow you are to anger tells a significant story. We have much to learn from conflict.

Chapter 8

Help Others Around You to Develop Personal Accountability

There are two ways of spreading light: to be the candle or
the mirror that reflects it.
Edith Wharton

AT ONE TIME, the terminals that we had across the United States were operating under what I labeled the "Burger King Model." Each unit was stand-alone, doing its job under the "Have It Your Way" mantra. This side of our business was evolving into a hodge-podge of widely varied procedures, reporting mechanisms, execution strategies, and accountabilities. Each terminal was even beginning to develop its own unique language and culture. It was a real Tower of Babel. And it was getting out of control. . . .

We carefully studied the situation and came to the conclusion that such a patchwork was not in the best long-term interests of the organization. A new, standardized system was to be created and implemented. Fundamental to this change was the introduction of a standardized scorecard for our terminal superintendents and their people. We were going to make managing by accountability the way things got done.

I remember the conference call we had with our folks to an-
nounce the new approach. The response was not very upbeat,
to say the least. One superintendent's comments struck me in
particular.

He actually said, with all of his peers and superiors listening in, that such an accountability-based approach would make
things worse, not better. He went on to add that the inevitable
"combat"—and he used the word "combat"—which would certainly follow from his subordinates now being held accountable
would create more problems than they would solve.

I think every now and then about what he said and realize how
off base he was. Being driven by the natural fear that comes when
one considers conflict, he had assumed the worst-case scenario
and moved right to preparing for a combat assault.

Certainly managing by accountability makes conflict pro-
bable—and, in many cases, inevitable. However, assuming combat
is also a given is simply wrong. Combat is an option.

Accountability to others serves as a monitor of our own accountability pulse. It helps us to better understand how our personal accountability measures up. However, as sensitive, self-serving creatures, we sometimes chafe under another's accountability simply
because we're full of pride. Other times, we chafe because we sense
that something other than constructive guidance is being offered.

I'm convinced the superintendent on the conference call was
concerned about two things in particular: first was that he was
now going to be an "open book" and didn't feel it necessary. His
pride was saying, "I am doing a great job here. My boss knows it.
I believe my subordinates know it. Why do I need to be further
scrutinized?"

Second, he was worried what his subordinates would think
when he had to do the same thing to them that now was being
done to him. He was scared they would hold him in contempt,

as he felt his superiors were now doing to him. He was taking it personally and getting combative.

In my experience, this kind of thinking is not uncommon. In a Charlie Brown cartoon, Lucy says, "You, Charlie Brown, are a foul ball in the line drive of life. You stand in the shadow of your own goal post. You are a miscue. You are three putts on the eighteenth green. You are a seven-ten split in the tenth frame. You're a missed free throw, a called third strike. You are a dropped rod-and-reel in the lake of life. Do you understand me, Charlie Brown? Have I made myself clear?"

A lot of people have a Lucy in their life. Many times it is a lousy boss who has stolen their confidence and their thunder. People with this kind of baggage are often the ones who fight accountability at every turn. And, from a self-preservation point of view, they are probably right. Nevertheless, however bad they had been treated in the past is not a justification for ducking accountability. It doesn't absolve them of the responsibilities they are entrusted with. It may sound hard-hearted. But if someone is not facing themselves in the mirror everyday and having others do the same to them, then they shouldn't be in leadership positions. Nobody put a gun to their head and said, "You must be a manager." With every position comes choice and accountability. If they choose to take the job, then they must also accept wholeheartedly the accountability that comes with it—regardless what has happened before. Its really that simple.

The Importance of Scorecards

As our company moved forward to reshape the terminals into a more singular structure with a focus on accountability, it was incumbent upon me to first explain to our people why all this was happening and then be certain the execution met the accountability objective. The route I chose was to implement a scorecard system.

I am a big fan of scorecards. The transparency that comes from effectively using scorecards leaves no doubt as to whether the person is right or not for the job. It makes the job of a leader much easier because those who consistently perform below average are very much aware of it.

Like the batting average in baseball, which is the purest scorecard I know of, these low-output folks often put pressure on themselves either to improve, look for another job, or take early retirement. In any case, the ability of the leader is enhanced because potential obstacles in the form of human resources crises are many times averted.

Moreover, the high-output folks are also aware that the low-output ones have been put on notice without any insults or personal attacks, aka combat. This further expands the credibility of the manager in the eyes of his or her achievers. It makes managing by accountability less difficult to accomplish.

Scorecards and Balance

If executed properly, the scorecard method will make it quite clear how someone is doing. This is easier said than done. I remember a "Weekly Reader" cartoon when I was a kid:

A boy had lost his nickel and was looking for it on the street. When asked by a passerby what he was doing, the boy replied he was searching for the nickel that he had lost over there—pointing across the street. When the passerby told him that he was looking in the wrong place, the boy said, "I know. But the light is better over here."

In most businesses, people live and die by the numbers on their scorecard. For many of these numbers, there are trade-offs that have to or should be made for the good and betterment of the manager's own department or the good of the company. I have seen many aspiring leaders deal away their credibility because they manage to their numbers at all cost, even when it is obvious that the decision is detrimental to the greater good.

I have had people publicly state that they know the right thing to do is X but state that they're going to do Y because of their "numbers." They are worried about themselves and what others will think—nothing else. They are obviously not worried about those around them who can see this very clearly. How can they respect this individual who only hold themselves accountable to numbers on a piece of paper? They really can't.

Scorecards need to be looking for the right things in the right places. And, they have to be right for the overall benefit of the organization. They have to be balanced. If out of kilter even a little, scorecards can render the fallacy, "the operation was successful, but the patient died," as true.

Mistakes Made When It Comes to Scorecards

Some common mistakes that are made when seeking to create scorecards that empower management by accountability include getting way too personal when it comes to criticism; ignoring problems in the hope they will go away; and, over praising.

Getting Way Too Personal in Criticism

Over the years, I have collected some of the more memorable quotes from scorecards that have passed by me. Ask yourself if any, some, or all of these cross the line between professional and personal:

"Since my last report, he has reached rock bottom and has started to dig."

"His men would follow him anywhere, but only out of morbid curiosity."

"This guy slipped into the gene pool when no one was looking."

"This employee is really not so much of a has-been, but more of a definitely won't be."

"Works well when under constant supervision and cornered like a rat in a trap."

"When she opens her mouth, it seems that this is only to change whichever foot was previously in there."

"He would be out of his depth in a parking lot puddle."

"This young lady has delusions of adequacy."

"She sets low personal standards and then consistently fails to achieve them."

"This employee should go far—and the sooner he starts, the better."

"This employee is depriving a village somewhere of an idiot."

"A gross ignoramus—144 times worse than an ordinary ignoramus."

"When his I.Q. reaches 50, he should sell."

"She donated her brain to science before she was finished using it."

"If you give him a penny for his thoughts, you'd get change."

We need to make sure that any comments which are made as the results of scorecards are not done to ridicule or berate other people. Managing by accountability demands the highest level of integrity in all that we say and how we say it.

Ignore Problems in the Hope They Will Go Away

Hope is one of the greatest of all human traits. Without hope, life has little or no meaning. When it comes to managing people, an effective leader is grounded in the responsibilities they are charged with, and with the hope that progress can be attained. In many situations, because managers want to believe that the people under them can do better, glaring problems are ignored. Reality is replaced with hope. This is tough. We don't want to be cruel. We want to think the best in most people. That they can turn it around. Change. Improve. But there are times when it is necessary to cut someone loose.

The Cleveland Browns is one of the storied franchises in the history of professional football. An original member of the National Football League, Cleveland won four NFL championships and reached the title game six other times during the 1950s and '60s. During those years, future Hall-of-Famers like Jim Brown, Otto Graham, and Leroy Kelly made their mark and built huge fan followings in both Cleveland and around the country.

However, if you ask most Browns fans today who their favorite player ever is, it is Bernie Kosar. The local boy who won a National Championship as quarterback for the University of Miami and returned home to lead the Browns to the playoffs throughout the late 1980s stands above the other greats in team history.

In 1991, the Browns hired Bill Belichick, the now-three-time Super Bowl winner, as coach. Unlike the fans of Cleveland, Belichick was not a huge fan of Kosar. After a 29-14 loss to Denver in week 8, the Browns released Kosar. Belichick told a press conference Kosar was suffering from "diminishing skills." Shockwaves rippled throughout football-crazy Cleveland. Many said the unthinkable had happened.

Despite all the hype, the coach was right; Kosar's performance had trailed off in recent years. Still the release of the popular player set off a wave of anger among Browns fans, some of whom came to the next home game in Kosar masks. Belichick was eventually run out of town and later ended up in New England, where he built a dynasty.

Belichick was and continues to manage by accountability, despite the passion, allegiance, and love fans feel for their favorite players. His ability to see through the emotion and look squarely at the outputs has made him one of the most effective coaches in NFL history.

Overpraising

I like what Emily Post said when she observed, "An overdose of praise is like 10 lumps of sugar in coffee; only a very few people can swallow it." It is critical to tell people when they are doing a good job. We all seek praise from those whom we value: a boss, our parents, our spouses. But praise should be something that is treated with the highest amount of respect. Overkill on praise can ultimately lead to whacked-out expectations and confusion.

Some Guidelines for an Effective Scorecard

The ultimate decision of how to conduct a scorecard system is up to each company and the people who lead it. Performance evaluations are intended to measure the extent to which the employee's performance meets the requirements of a particular position and to establish goals for the future; strengthen the relationship between you and the employee; open up channels of communication; appraise past performance; recognize good performance; identify areas that might require improvement; enable yourself to assess your own communication and supervisory skills.

To help set parameters, I've included the following guidelines to help leaders better implement their scorecards. They highlight some strengths and weaknesses I have observed over the years.

Is the Scorecard Easy to Read and Understand?

The portion of a good scorecard that deals with performance is concise and written in plain language that any member of the organization can readily understand. There is a manageable number of performance indicators (goals and measures) that are clearly stated so that any member of the organization can understand their significance. In addition, the overall benefits that the organization achieves from the employee doing the scorecard are clearly presented

Potential problem areas that may arise include a multitude of performance indicators that require a voluminous performance section to cover; lengthy, text-heavy narratives with limited use of tables and graphics (people like pictures!); and, complicated numbering of goals and measures. When it doubt, keep it simple!

Are the Performance Data Valid, Verifiable, and Timely?

A good scorecard provides data sources for each reported indicator and discloses any results that are missing for a significant number of indicators due to lagging data. Be sure that the scorecard describes data verification and validation efforts as well as data sources for individual indicators.

Are the Goals and Objectives of the Scorecard Stated as Outcomes?

To the greatest extent practical, long-term (strategic) goals and annual performance goals are expressed as measurable end outcomes or at least intermediate outcomes that a lay reader can readily understand and relate to tangible benefits. Where strategic goals are stated at a high level of generality, they are accompanied by strategic objectives that provide more specific and measurable outcomes. Good scorecards also capture all of an organization's key missions.

Potential problem areas here may be that many goals are stated as activities or outputs rather than outcomes. Or, goals are stated as outcomes, but too vaguely or at too high a level of generality to permit realistic measurement or attribution of results to the person's efforts. And, individual goals are not clearly tied to organizational benefits.

Does the Scorecard Show How the Person's Results Will Make the Organization Better?

The key ingredients in a successful evaluation are as follows: identifying job standards; being consistent in measuring and communicating the extent to which whose standards are being met; and providing opportunities for feedback and clarification.

Does the Scorecard Explain Failures to as to Why the Person Failed to Achieve Their Goals?

The explanation of shortfalls should include a description of planned actions to remedy them in the future, thereby adding to the reader's understanding of the shortfall and the reader's confidence that the shortfall is being seriously addressed. In situations where confusion arises, the scorecard does not clearly disclose all performance shortfalls. Either shortfalls are not specifically disclosed or the report must be read closely to find them.

Does the Scorecard Offer Suggestions for Growth and Improvement?

No effective scorecard can be considered complete without some discussion and assessment of the employee's potential for professional and career growth.

Fostering Accountability

Effective leaders recognize the need to help others around them embark on a journey of personal accountability. Inherent in that is fostering the right environment for personal accountability to take root. Here are four ways to proceed.

Welcome It

We can work to avoid being defensive when people offer suggestions, maintaining an open ear for feedback. When we protect ourselves with defense mechanisms, we become hard, which is too steep a price to pay.

Model It

Holding others accountable requires a willingness to confront others with some difficult truths. At the same time, it models to others how they can hold themselves accountable as well.

Use Opportunities to Teach about Accountability

We can talk about what we are doing and why—providing insight as to what is going on to those who might be confused.

Never Question People's Motives

Accusations are like weapons of mass destruction; they destroy the entire area in a scorched-earth kind of way. When we wonder what's driving others, we can say, "I may be wrong, but it looks to me like so-and-so happened. Tell me how you're feeling about it." When we refuse to question others' motives, they are less likely to question ours.

Chapter 9

Putting It All Together

We must not promise what we ought not, lest we be called
on to perform what we cannot.
Abraham Lincoln

TO BE ACCOUNTABLE, one demands a promise and an obligation to fulfill an acceptance of the consequence or outcome, positive or negative. It is, therefore, not unreasonable to expect leaders to be responsible for the consequences of their actions to the stakeholders and communities in which they operate.

In today's borderless environment, accountability principles are paramount to everybody's interest. The right to know—whether businesses act in an entirely accountable way, or whether their actions will have profound implications on public interests—is embedded as part of the accountability concept.

Indeed, many organizations have already moved in this direction—they are becoming transparent, accountable, and fulfilling their new roles with public interest at the heart of their business strategy. The debate is not whether the purpose of business is business but rather, whether it recognizes the need of corporations to be accountable to their stakeholders and community at large. Such responsibility is no longer seems to be an option. If this is true, then we have to get away from thinking that there is more than one version of the truth. The truth must be treated as absolute and singular.

Words Matter

Words matter. Not as much as actions. But they do matter.

David Mamet's play Glengarry Glen Ross, which also became a hit movie, is a scathing attack on how words can get obfuscated in American business. The only characters whom we do not witness in some attempt to steal from, cheat, or trick one of the others are both extremely meek men who, it is implied, do not have much chance at great success.

The sales office setting serves as a microcosm of truthlessness: as the top man gets a Cadillac and the bottom man gets fired, every man must not only work for his own success but also hope for—or actively engineer—his coworkers' failure. It is management by attrition: I move up when you move down. The system is brutal and compassionless.

Throughout the play, different characters use the word "talk" (or variations of it) to imply idle chatter that is not supported by action. One salesman tells another that what he learned in business school is "talk"; another tries to figure out if his coworker is serious about robbing the office or if he is just "talking"; another tells a customer that his wife's insistence on canceling their deal is just something that she "said," not something that they have to actually do.

In every case, characters use this terminology in an attempt to undermine the "talk" in question. Whenever someone does not want to accept the reality of what is being said, they make an accusation of "talk." The would-be-thief cleverly suggests that he himself is just "talking" about the break-in until he feels that his verbal trap—to force his coworker to commit the robbery—is set.

At that point, he reveals that he has actually been "talking" about the break-in. The word is the same but his tone switches the word "talk" itself from meaningless to meaningful.

Similarly, in the real world we too often find there is an overemphasis on words rather than the whole truth. Throughout my career, I have found these phrases to be particularly vexing when it comes to lack of dignity in using words:

"I know you don't want to hear this, but . . ."

"I might get fired for saying this, but . . ."

"To be honest with you . . ."

Each of these sayings undermine the credibility of the person saying them. Words represent us. They need to be treated accordingly. Think about the opening of the Bible: "In the beginning was the word. . . ."

Some Final Thoughts

Those who manage by accountability viscerally know that external rules cannot substitute for character. That holding oneself accountable is an acquirement—like music, like a foreign language, like poker. Nobody is born with it. Managing by accountability evolves over time within us.

There always exists a temptation when things don't go well to hide from responsibility and point fingers of blame away from ourselves. We all did it as children and many of us have never lost the trait.

Having completed this book, I have to assume that you want to break away from that immature mindset to do things differently. And I salute you. However, a piece of advice from someone who has tried throughout his career to manage by accountability— at times very well and at others quite poorly: be patient with yourself and don't ever quit trying to do the right things for the right reasons.

It is easy to set low expectations of yourself. You'll never be disappointed. . . .

It is tempting to forsake integrity as your guiding principle. You'll always be ready for the grey areas. . . .

It is much simpler to speak of action rather than to act. There is little risk of failure if you don't do anything. . . .

It is natural to run away from conflict and change. This way everybody will like you. . . .

It is good to be known as a nice guy. . . . Holding others to account makes life too complicated.

This is all true, unless you want to be a results-driven leader.

Managing by accountability is the greatest challenge any leader will ever undertake. To hold themselves up for others to see. To take responsibility when it is needed. To accept change and the conflict it brings. To make it happen.

The rewards are clear: credibility, effectiveness, the opportunity to have your people accomplish wonderful things, and an inner satisfaction that is priceless. I conclude with words from Marcus Aurelius, written nearly two thousand years ago:

> If thou workest at that which is before thee, following right reason seriously, vigorously, calmly, without allowing anything else to distract thee but keeping thy divine part pure, if thou shouldst be bound to give it back immediately, if thou holdest to this, expecting nothing, fearing nothing, but satisfied with thy present activity according to nature and with heroic truth in every word and sound which thou utterest, thou wilt live happily. And there is no man who is able to prevent this.

Notes

Chapter 1: The Mandate of Accountability

1. *The Nikkei Weekly*, 12/13/2004 Edition.

2. Gareth Bladon and Kerry Cronin, "Accountability, responsibility must be defined," *Business Day*, Management Review Edition, February 27, 2006, Opinion & Editorial, p. 8.

Chapter 5: Live the Integrity Imperative

1. Warren E. Buffett, "Who really cooks the books?" *The New York Times*, July 24, 2002.

Chapter 7: Accept Inevitable Change and Conflict and Accountability's Role

1. Robert Lacey. *Ford: The Man and the Machine* (New York: Little Brown & Co, 1996.

2. Peter Vail. *Spirited Leading and Learning: Process Wisdom for a New Age* (New York: Jossey-Bass, 1998).

Recommended Reading

Bennett, William J. *The Book of Virtues* (Simon & Schuster, 1993) New York.

Bennis, Warren and Burt Nanus. *Leaders: The Strategies for Taking Charge* (Harper & Row, 1985) New York.

Bossidy, Larry. *Execution: The Discipline of Getting Things Done* (Crown Books, 2002) New York.

Burns, James MacGregor. *Leadership* (Harper & Row, 1978) New York.

Chamberlain, Joshua Lawrence. *Bayonet Forward: My Civil War Reminiscences* (Stan Clark Books, 1994) Gettysburg, PA.

Ciulla, Joanne B., ed. *Ethics, The Heart of Leadership* (Quorum Books, 1998) Westport, CT.

Cleveland, Harlan. *Leadership and the Information Revolution* (World Academy of Art & Science, 1997) Minneapolis, MN.

D'Este, Carlo. *Eisenhower* (Henry Holt, 2002) New York.

———. *Patton: A Genius for War* (Harper Collins, 1992) New York.

Goleman, Daniel. *Working With Emotional Intelligence* (Bantam Books, 1998) New York.

Greenleaf, Robert K. *Servant Leadership* (Paulist Press, 1977) Mahwah, NJ.

Heifetz, Ronald A. *Leadership without Easy Answers* (Harvard University Press, 1994) Cambridge, MA.

Kelley, Robert E. *The Power of Followership: How to Create Leaders People Want to Follow, and Followers Who Lead Themselves* (Doubleday Currency, 1992) New York.

McCullough, David. *1776* (Simon & Schuster, 2005) New York.

———. *Truman* (Simon & Schuster, 1992) New York.

———. *The Path between the Seas* (Simon & Schuster, 1977) New York.

Oates, Stephen. *With Malice Toward None: A Life of Abraham Lincoln* (Harper, 1994) New York.

Pelfrey, William. *Billy, Alfred, and General Motors* (AMACOM, 2006) New York.

Rost, Joseph C. *Leadership for the Twenty-First Century* (Praeger, 1991) Westport, CT.

Wren, J. Thomas, ed. *The Leader's Companion: Insights on Leadership through the Ages* (Free Press, 1995) New York.

Index

About the Authors

M. DAVID DEALY is Senior Vice President of Transportation for Burlington Northern Santa Fe Railroad. A nearly 30-year veteran of railroad management, he has served in top-level positions in operations and marketing throughout the industry, as well as serving on the boards of several companies and non-profits, including the National Alzheimer's Association. With Andrew Thomas, he is author of *Defining the Really Great Boss* (Praeger, 2004) and *Change or Die* (Praeger, 2005).

ANDREW R. THOMAS is Assistant Professor of Marketing and International Business and Director of the Center for Organizational Development at The University of Akron. A successful global entrepreneur, he has conducted business in more than 120 countries. A *New York Times* best-selling author, his books include *Global Manifest Destiny and Aviation Insecurity*, and, with M. David Dealy, *Defining the Really Great Boss* (Praeger, 2004) and *Change or Die* (Praeger, 2005). He is also co-editor of *Direct Marketing in Action* (Praeger, 2006).

.